Career Hacks

from 10 Digital Ladies 2017 Awards-winners,

event speakers and community.

ELCOME TO THE 10 DIGITAL LADIES BOOK OF CAREER HACKS.

10 Digital Ladies is a networking group that supports women in digital who want to further their careers and develop their own version of success. Now in our fourth year, our membership consists of almost 1,500 mid- to senior -level women in tech.

We stand for the principle that success is personal. For some women this may mean reaching the board, for others it may be having a portfolio career or being a specialist in product or engineering. And for some it will be about finding the right balance between work and play.

We aim to provide inspiration, support and practical tips to our community and beyond. Last year we decided to increase our impact and ran our first ever awards event, sponsored by EY. This year we set our ambitions higher with an even bigger awards ceremony - thanks to the support of Equal Experts, NHS Digital and Wavemaker - and our first ever book of career hacks. The fact that you are reading this is thanks to the generosity of our book sponsors Wavemaker and Photobox.

Why do we exist?

In the UK tech sector, the number of women working in IT and computing represent just 15-17 per cent of the total. Enabling women to meet their full potential in work could add as much as $28 trillion to our annual GDP in 2025. 'Nuff said.

How do you eat an elephant?

We don't claim that we'll change the world – although we're trying. The numbers above describe an elephantine task and we know there's much to do, both to promote diversity in general (not just gender diversity), and also work in partnership with men, not against or without them. The only way to attack an elephantine task is bit by bit, so we want to do our bit to give digital women a place to share stories and inspire each other.

So why write a book?

Over the past four years we have had the privilege of hearing from hundreds of inspirational women who've attended and spoken at our events. Again and again we have been struck by the incredible honesty of our participants, as well as by how much their career hacks resonate with our audience.

We think there is real value in sharing these tips - the advice you'll read here is simply not replicated in management manuals and magazines elsewhere. The hacks in this book come not only from last year's award winners and panelists, but also from our 10 Digital Ladies network. We're enormously grateful for the incredible response we had from our community - 100 pages was not enough for us to include every single contribution. A big thank you to everyone who got in touch - we acknowledge you in the closing pages of this book and we hope to find other ways to share your tips on other platforms in future.

Our goal is to empower and inspire, be practical and appeal to individual ideas of success. We hope the pages of this book will do that for you, and more.

Enjoy!

The 10 Digital Ladies Co-Founders

Lucia Adams, Business Transformation Consultant and Coach

Sally Foote, Product Director

Nina Lovelace, Digital Product Consultant and Entrepreneur

Laila Edy, Digital Product Specialist and Coach

Huge thanks to Laura Oliver, Freelance Journalist, Editor and Digital Consultant who edited this book. Laura writes and edits articles for a range of news titles and helps media organisations, from the FT to the BBC, train staff and develop strategies for better audience engagement. She's helped us work with our community to source hacks for this book and produce its chapters. And thank you to Leigh Furby, Designer at Photobox, who has made it all come to life so beautifully.

It's our first book so it's been a big learning curve for us all - Laura and Leigh brought creativity and flair, as well as humility and patience as we battled with deadlines and new learning experiences!

A note from Wavemaker who generously sponsored the editing and creation of this book:

"In the future, there will be no female leaders. There will just be leaders." But until Sheryl Sandberg's words come true, we need initiatives like 10 Digital Ladies to help drive change and inspire women to shape their own vision of career success.

At Wavemaker, we're committed to building a culture that promotes and celebrates diversity. We want to lead the way within our industry and beyond in this arena and for that reason, I'm both proud and excited to be supporting 10 Digital Ladies and this book.

Career success is and should be up to everyone to define for themselves, but having a good role model in your life will help you express your true self. Women need to see other women step up and take charge of their own careers. The hacks in this book are not only a catalogue of ideas but also the encouraging words of a hundred role models: How to find your voice, how to define what success looks like to you, how to be the best version of yourself. They cement the point that a career path might be an individual choice but no one is alone on the road. Use these tips from the women that came before you as an inspiration and a guide. You are not alone. There's a whole community of Digital Ladies (and at least one man) ready to support you.

My 7-year-old daughter recently came to me and confidently stated that when she grows up, she wants to be an artist, a teacher or a YouTuber. I'm thinking that thanks to initiatives like 10 Digital Ladies, she might grow up to become all three things - and be very happy and fulfilled in her career.

James Edgar

Chief Talent Officer, Market Development, Wavemaker

A note from Photobox who generously sponsored the printing and delivery of this book:

photob★x

Photobox is proud to sponsor 10 Digital Ladies and the work they do developing and supporting the tech community in London. There are not enough women in tech and as an industry we suffer for it.

I'm encouraged to see the level of focus on STEM and active inclusion at my 4 year old daughter's school and I'm hopeful that by the time her generation enters the workforce they will not have to contend with many of the gender and sexual identity issues we face today.

However, that future won't just happen. We all have a lot of work to do to ensure that it does.

With the increasing momentum of #metoo, Gender Pay Gap, and LGBTIQ initiatives, it is a challenging but exciting time in the world of work that fills us with hope for the future. 10 Digital Ladies provides an invaluable support network for our female leaders as they help us all navigate the road ahead.

Dave Wascha

Chief Product Officer - Photobox Group

Launching a successful start-up

"I think it's a common misconception that people from an arts and creative background wouldn't be able to set up a commercial, tech company. The training that I had enabled me to think bigger, break down barriers and not be afraid to disrupt."

Emily Forbes

10 Digital Ladies Entrepreneur Award winner 2017

Emily Forbes is the Founder and CEO of Seenit, a video collaboration tool that enables companies to produce high impact video at scale by engaging their own communities of employees, customers and fans around the world.

LAUNCHING YOUR OWN DIGITAL START-UP MAY SEEM DAUNTING BUT with the right support and confidence in your entrepreneurial abilities you can find success. You'll need to trust in your idea and instincts and build the right team around you - from mentors and investors through to employees. What they bring to the business needs to complement you and your vision.

To introduce our hacks for a successful start-up here's some advice from a 10 Digital Ladies event featuring award-winner Emily Forbes alongside:

Natasha Pilbrow, a former film lawyer and now Co-Founder and COO of LeSalon, a premium beauty booking app that provides services where you are, and at the same time empowers women in the beauty industry.

Matilde Giglio, Co-Founder and CMO at Compass News: the Spotify for journalism offering diverse, high-quality, pay-walled newspapers at a single-subscription price.

Gabriela Hersham, Founder and CEO of co-working start-up Huckletree, a "physical" business in a digital world.

Target the right investors, the ones who 'get' your vision and can also lend support, whether that's property investors who can give you space to work in, or can bring more than money to the table.

Someone once told Emily Forbes: "If you ask for money, you'll get advice; if you ask for advice, you'll get money." You need to build relationships with investors so that what they offer is on your terms.

Co-founders need to share your passion and the workload. If they're not operational, things can be imbalanced, leading to stress and upset later. A true partner can change your life.

Stay positive when times get tough. Any new business has challenging times, so developing resilience and a growth mindset is crucial.

"In a start-up situation when everyone is freaking out and worried the money is going to run out, keep calm and carry on. Work hard, focus on the goal, something always comes up - the darkest hours are those just before dawn"

Hannah Bowden

Programme Director

"If I didn't give up my job to work on my start-up, it would always stay a side hustle. A year after working full time on my start-up I had to take on a part-time job. Has my start-up now gone back to being nothing more than a side hustle? No. My part-time job is my side hustle to fund and grow my start-up."

Laura Robinson

Founder and Creative Director

"Trying to do everything yourself is sabotaging your own success. When the to-do list starts to pile up, ask yourself: which of these things can I delegate or get support with?"

Flora Graham

Science Journalist

"Create a personal brand. Personal branding is the practice of people marketing (or selling) themselves and their careers as brands - the ongoing process of building a defined image or impression in the mind of others about an individual."

Tiffany Charters

Business Coach for Mum Entrepreneurs

How to create
and manage change

"When faced with a big decision to pivot your career, ask three people you trust about it - your partner, a work colleague who knows you really well and whom you trust, your best friend, a mentor etc. Having an external point of view might raise some questions you hadn't thought of to help weigh the pros and cons."

Bénédicte Autret

10 Digital Ladies Agent for Change Award winner 2017

Bénédicte Autret is Head of Strategic Relationships for News & Publishers in the UK & Benelux at Google.

HEN IT COMES TO AFFECTING CHANGE IN YOUR CAREER OR WITHIN an organisation, there are plenty of pitfalls to avoid, not least the stress that taking that first step can often bring. Transformations vary but lessons can be shared across contexts: others will have experienced similar challenges. Helping us understand how to be a good agent for change, award-winner Bénédicte Autret and the following changemakers have inspired these hacks:

Jodie Rogers is HR Business Partner at MEC, where she ran the "Brave Your Bias" programme about unconscious bias. Her passion has always been to positively impact people's experiences and for this to extend beyond the office.

Kim Matenchuk is Senior Director for Food & Beverage/Consumer Package Goods at GE Digital. She previously spent 9 years at Google working with companies such as Sky and Thomas Cook on their digital advertising strategies.

Anna Carus-Wilson co-runs Frank Partners, where she helps a range of clients improve their communication skills. She is very curious about people, especially what makes them tick and, naturally, how they communicate.

Use silence as an effective tool especially when you disagree with someone. They will have to go through the process of trying to work out what you are thinking while you get some more time to think through your response.

When answering a question, think about how someone else would behave when answering it. How might a colleague you admire answer and what might you learn from their tone and language?

To help overcome imposter syndrome, preparation can make a big difference. Speak to people who boost your confidence before you do something scary - it will help you get into a more positive mindset.

Break down your overall career goal into its component parts and, for each one, recognise what your 'must achieve' and 'must avoid' criteria are in order to understand where you can be flexible. This technique allows you to go into a negotiation prepared for whatever the other party might offer you.

"All too often people speak before they think, think and then don't speak or speak but then don't act. Take your time to think through what impact you want your words, and ultimately actions, to have, then follow through with conviction. Actions deliver your words which transmit your intentions."

Lindsay Ratcliffe

Director of Innovation and Design

"Keep asking for the things you want -
a promotion, a pay rise, business trips,
flexible working - whatever it is. You should
never leave your bosses guessing what it is
you are after - it could lead to others getting
an opportunity that could have been yours."

Inga Thordar

Executive Editor

"Find a colleague in the role above your own whom you know and trust. Take them to coffee or lunch so you can learn how they got promoted, successfully negotiated pay raises etc. Every organization is different; knowing how to advance within your own is invaluable."

Lauren Maffeo

Senior Content Analyst

"Get really good at asking yourself and others two questions: what did I do well and what could I have done better? Reflecting on feedback little and often is your greatest weapon."

Kate Thompson

Developing
your career

"Digital careers are crying out for women. I don't think women should shy away from starting something because they don't feel they know everything about that particular career. It's just a really great journey to go on that learning challenge."

Priya Lakhani OBE

10 Digital Ladies Newcomer Award winner 2017

Priya Lakhani OBE is the Founder CEO of CENTURY Tech. A former libel barrister, Priya founded FMCG business Masala Masala in 2008 to address the lack of ready-made ethnic sauces available at nationwide retailers. Her transition to digital followed a similar problem-solving approach: after becoming aware of the number of children underperforming in UK schools, Priya founded CENTURY Tech in 2014 with the goal of disrupting the education sector by utilising big data and data mining techniques to improve students' learning outcomes.

TAKING CONTROL OF HOW YOUR CAREER DEVELOPS IS OFTEN EASIER said than done. Creating new opportunities for yourself or welcoming the chance to learn and master new skills are good places to start. Silencing your doubting inner critic can be the biggest barrier of all but embracing the new can take you in unexpected directions - or into entirely new careers, as Priya Lakhani's story shows.

Inspired by Priya, Catherine Knivett and Laurie Higdon, how can you hack your career development?

Catherine Knivett is Head of Partnerships at the Corsham Institute and former Head of Digital Skills Policy at the Greater London Authority. She led the Mayor of London's Digital Talent Programme, which aims to increase the number of women and ethnic minority Londoners joining the technology workforce.

Laurie Higdon, Talent Acquisition Manager at Join the Dots and former Recruitment Manager at Dentsu Aegis Network. Her work has given her insight into what characterises digital talent as well as tips for non-techies looking to hire or collaborate with digital specialists.

If you don't feel you're getting the opportunities you warrant, don't hang around. There's a shortage of women in digital and you deserve to be fought for. This isn't about ultimatums but valuing yourself: be clear about what you expect from an employer and don't stay somewhere that doesn't feel right.

When Priya Lakhani wants to get something done she imagines 'putting a picture in her museum'. She thinks about what achievements she wants to leave as a legacy and uses this to stay on track and overcome obstacles and detractors.

You won't find everything you need in a single mentor; you need to have a network of people from which you can learn different things. These people don't always have to be senior to you or even in the same specialist field.

Know your personal story and be able to tell it to others. Being able to articulate why you do what you do is a way to attract talent and set a company culture from the beginning.

"Every time you hear yourself or someone else telling you 'you can't do this' or 'you can't say that' or 'you must wait' think to yourself: 'If I don't rail against this voice now I am holding not just myself but all future generations of women back.' Then go ahead and prove them wrong."

Tessa Cooper

Director of People

"Get inspired by others. Find people who have achieved what you're after, or done something you admire. Note how they talk about their role, check out their career steps, the experience and skills that they call out, and reach out to them to grab a coffee - LinkedIn, Twitter and personal websites can be very useful."

Magda Lechowicz

Innovation Consultant and Service Designer

"When you start a new job or even a new position in your current company, remember that new-job nervousness is a good thing. Let your voice be heard, ask questions and repeat what your understanding of the solution is out loud. Understand that to be corrected isn't a criticism, it's to help you improve and will ultimately help broaden your knowledge."

Flora Okumagba

Agile Project Manager

"Find a mentor/coach early in and throughout your career: someone you can confide in, that has your interests in mind, who can guide you, someone you can learn from and who has walked a similar path to you."

Sarah Arnold

Founder and Director

Being a
non-executive director

"Get board experience somewhere. Start smaller, join the board of a charity, join the board of governors of your local school - do something that's useful and that talks to you but that will give you board experience. Just start - don't aim right for the end."

Claudia Arney

10 Digital Ladies Non-Executive Director Award winner 2017

Claudia Arney has extensive experience, both in executive and non-executive roles, in transforming traditional businesses and capitalising on the opportunities offered by the digital revolution. Claudia is currently a non-executive director for Aviva, Derwent London plc, Halfords Group plc and the Premier League.

THE BIGGEST PROBLEM WITH GETTING YOUR FIRST GIG AS A NON-executive director is that everyone wants you to already have experience of the role. Then whether you're in your first or tenth NED role, the challenges keep rolling.

In this chapter, our hacks are inspired by the words of award-winner Claudia Arney as well as:

Marina Gorey is Co-Founder and Chief of Staff at SuperAwesome, the largest media platform in the world for kids, and has worked with teams in the London, New York and remote "Techstars Everywhere" programmes. Her mentoring role helps expedite business growth and support entrepreneurs.

Ann Holman is a Board-level Director, Non-Executive Director and Digital Strategy Consultant. She is a Partner at Neu Design, Co-Founder of Holbirt, and a Non-Executive Director at Vivo Life.

Shelley Facius is Non-Executive Director of ExLabs, a software development company. She has worked in tech since the early 1990s in marketing and communications.

Understand what's in it for you: you have to find ways to elevate yourself beyond your current role; being a non-executive director is about progression, it's about extending out of your comfort zone.

As a non-executive director, your job is to ask the right questions and challenge the answers. When you're offering advice to the chief executive or board, the more you can root it in your own experience the more credible it sounds, and the more memorable it is.

Work out how much time you can commit to as well as what you can offer and for what companies you'd be a good fit. Most public limited company boards will contract you for around 30 days per year - in your mind, add 50% to that.

If you're a non-executive director, try to stay involved with a few smaller companies too so you can be hands on and learn what's changing for staff, businesses and technology from a different perspective.

Moving from doing to advising can be a challenge: in this role it's not your company to run; you are there to help and facilitate. If you are someone who prefers to be hands-on then this might not be for you.

"You know more than you think! Back yourself; if you didn't deserve to be there, you wouldn't be."

Camille Peetroons

Commercial and Data Product Manager

"The digital industry is rewarding and exciting but to make it happen and succeed you have to be ambitious and not afraid to ask for that pay rise or promotion. You also have to take responsibility for making your own opportunities."

Abba Newbery

Chief Marketing Officer

How to
manage a varied career

"I feel very in charge of my own career and my own choices which is very empowering and it makes everything much more fun. You can do the same thing but if you're choosing to do it and enjoying doing it, it will be a completely different experience from if you feel you've been forced to do it."

Zoe Cunningham

10 Digital Ladies Career Portfolioist Award winner 2017

Zoe Cunningham is Managing Director of Softwire and a film and theatre actor. Zoe has 16 years' experience working in the technology sector and in 2013 was named as one of the 100 most influential people in London's Tech City UK.

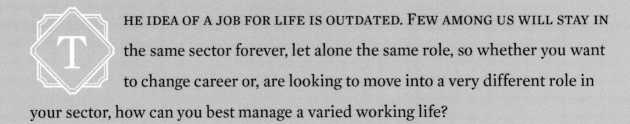

THE IDEA OF A JOB FOR LIFE IS OUTDATED. FEW AMONG US WILL STAY IN the same sector forever, let alone the same role, so whether you want to change career or, are looking to move into a very different role in your sector, how can you best manage a varied working life?

From "owning your career narrative" to making the leap into a new industry, these hacks based on a talk from 10 Digital Ladies' award winner Zoe Cunningham and the career portfolioists listed below will help you build your rich and varied career.

Aliceson Robinson is an Executive Director at Russell Reynolds Associates in the Consumer Sector, specializing in media and digital. She is a passionate advocate for philanthropy in the arts and sits on the Development Council for the Almeida Theatre. She is also a Trustee for the Royal Academy of Dance.

Vikki Coombes is in her fifth career having experienced 20 jobs across her previous four. She has studied for two degrees and nine professional qualifications so far and has lived in 11 urban centres across three countries. She is currently a transformational coach, learning leader, executive consultant and international public speaker.

Regularly check in on your priorities and make sure your timeline is right for you. A two-year 'forever horizon' might be more productive than a traditional five-year plan. Ask yourself what you are committed to and how you can do more of that and less of what disinterests you.

Don't readily accept how other people may pigeonhole you or define yourself so tightly that you create your own cage. Our strengths and weaknesses are likely to change over the course of our lives, unless we choose to hang onto them.

If you want to pursue multiple careers and are just starting out, it's very important to find the right balance between paid work and unpaid work. With paid work make sure it is a career which will progress and engage you rather than just being a support for your creative work.

Say no! 'No', or 'stop' or 'I'm going to do something different' are all affirmative statements; 'I don't want to do something' is a lot less powerful.

Being super organised is really important: "you can't just wake up and think 'what am I going to do today' — you need to plan your diary and schedule time for spontaneity and rest: give yourself permission to take time off.

"Mentors come in all shapes and sizes, don't limit yourself to the obvious candidates or to just one. I have several mentors who all have many different skill sets and experiences, and I go to them for different things. Also mentors are different than sponsors. You need both."

Reshma Shaikh

VP Strategy and Operations, COO

"Create a life plan before a career plan. Write a one page brief to yourself about all the things you want - life, family, friends, money, home, travel etc and then map your career to fit that. Not the other way around."

Melissa McVeigh

Product Director

"Be in charge of your story - especially if you've had a varied career across different types of roles, in different industries and in businesses at different stages, from start-ups to huge corporates. Finding the narrative thread that runs through your experience and weaving a story around that thread shows that you know your own strength, your own power."

Jane

"I've taken an interest in topics that were entirely perpendicular to my own. As well as providing context and broadening my expertise, it meant meeting folks who would look at some of the problems I had to solve in fresh, unexpected ways. My network of peers is much more diverse, and I think I've come to stand out for a broader understanding of my industry."

Ariane Bernard

Chief Digital Officer

How to be a "leader for good"

"Someone once told me you should develop future leaders not future followers and that's really stuck in my mind. My first few years of management were spent developing amazing people into mini-mes. Once I changed how I wanted to work with the people around me, develop my teams and embed those cultures and thought of people as future leaders, it really made a difference."

Amanda Neylon

10 Digital Ladies Leader for Good Award winner 2017

Amanda Neylon is Programme Director for Digital Delivery at NHS Digital, where she currently works helping the NHS develop its digital skills capacity. Amanda was previously Head of Digital at Macmillan Cancer Support and was responsible for all of the charity's online channels.

WHAT MAKES A GOOD LEADER - IS IT THEIR PERSONALITY, THEIR approach or their skills? Unsurprisingly, it's a combination of all these things, as well as the ability to look after themselves. In today's workplace, to be a "good" leader means going above and beyond, acting as a positive role model within a business, whether that's improving internal diversity, changing workplace culture or improving services for clients and customers.

With their backgrounds in the charity sector, where better to start than with hacks from an event featuring award-winner Amanda Neylon alongside:

Lara Burns, *Chief Digital and Technology Officer at Age UK, who has worked in the digital sector for 25 years, building her experience working in corporates, big agencies, freelance and now in the charity sector.*

Polly Cook, *Digital Transformation Programme Manager at the British Red Cross, who has more than eight years' experience working in digital within the charity sector. She previously led a team of agile project managers, delivering fundraising and volunteering products at Macmillan Cancer Support.*

Rebecca Cryan, *Senior Digital Editor at Macmillan Cancer Support. Her work in content and social roles in Macmillan's digital team has shown her that a good story is perhaps the most important thing you can have..*

Being successful shouldn't mean needing to have a 'work persona'. If you can't be yourself, is this the right organisation for you?

Invest in and look after yourself. This could be through coaching to help you distinguish between logical thoughts versus an internal critic, practicing self-kindness when you face challenges or growing your self-awareness to better understand your strengths. Taking care of yourself is important to avoid burnout and find success.

Make your vision digestible, make it clear what your top prioritises are, and then make it easy for your team to make things happen.

Be brave enough to build strong autonomous teams who can experiment and fail fast. This is as important in small businesses as it is at very large organisations. Unless you really empower people to just go and do stuff it's not going to work.

Use disruptive ways of working to break down silos and hierarchies by bringing people together in one room to focus on one problem.

"The greatest leaders and colleagues that I've worked with have consciously retained a sense of humility, no matter how senior their status or how much knowledge/ experience they have. The mantra 'good ideas can come from anywhere' depends on a team of open minds valuing everyone's opinion equally."

Lauren Murray
Consultant

"Giving clear and candid feedback in a respectful way is how you help your team flourish. If you're not saying what you need or expect from them in a way that they understand, they don't have the chance to improve. If you're telling other people what you wish someone would do, stop, and go tell the person you're talking about directly. Clear feedback is key."

Cheryl Clements

Performance Coach

"Be outward looking and know your network. Meet up with interesting people from other organisations regularly. If someone asks you to speak at an event and you can't, suggest another name from your network (and always think women/diversity first). Find others who have done the thing you are about to do and seek support."

Sarah Marshall

Head of Audience Growth

"Everyone, no matter how ambitious or driven, or personally committed to what they do for a living, can benefit from taking a step back and seeking balance. What that means for you will be unique and fluid. Go with what works for you, now. "

Penelope Jones

Coach and Consultant

"On hiring a team, surround yourself with great people from diverse backgrounds that share your values. Hire the people not the skills. The right person will always grow their skills. Team culture is key."

Stephanie Fletcher

Co-founder and Design Lead

It's hard for a woman to promote herself to others without sounding disingenuous, so find two other people whose abilities are as strong as your own - even if in a different area - and agree to promote each other's work, content and professional achievements.

Lexie Papaspyrou

Head of Academy

Being a
digital specialist

"I think I've achieved what I have because I've kept true to the core of me. I've never moved for a job title, I've never moved for a pay rise, I've never moved for a promotion. I've always moved because it's been the right kind of problem to solve or the right kind of organisation that's at the level I want to work with."

Lindsay Ratcliffe

10 Digital Ladies Specialist Award winner 2017

Lindsay Ratcliffe is Director of Customer Experience at HomeServe. She has dedicated her career to improving the experiences of customers across a huge range of industries including financial services, television, government, telecoms, utilities and manufacturing. She's the author of Agile Experience Design, which demonstrates how experience design combined with agile and lean methods can be can a strategic differentiator.

FOR MANY OF US IN DIGITAL CAREERS, IT CAN FEEL LIKE WE'RE FACED with a choice between taking on broader roles or remaining specialists within our chosen field. If you opt to be a specialist, how can you make that work for you? The first step, according to our community, is embracing what you know and what you don't. Just because you're an expert in one area doesn't mean you have to know everything.

Helping us understand what makes a great specialist and how we can hack our way to success are award-winner Lindsay Ratcliffe and:

Anne Simmons is a software engineer and Lead Consultant at Thoughtworks where she has spent the past eight years taking on increasingly senior roles, leading teams and coaching other developers. Anne now looks after building organisational and individual capabilities for ThoughtWorks' future capabilities.

Kate Rossiter is Marketing Controller for Entertainment Marketing Strategy & Planning at Sky where she manages the annual media strategy and spend, overall messaging lay-down and priorities, through to campaign performance.

Jo Holdaway is Chief Data Officer at ESI Media where she is focused the formulation and delivery of a business-wide data strategy for ESI. She is also the Chairman of the Association of Online Publishers.

Being a digital specialist means you can work in any sector. You're not expected to know every sector yourself, there will be other people in your team who are subject-matter experts or have years of sector experience.

It's important to have a network of people that share your specialism and who will support you but also give honest feedback. When you're taking a bold career step they can tell you if you are right to be scared or are being too self-critical.

Be empowered and excited by the fact the business don't understand as much as you do. Educate the business, no one else will fully understand. Digital is collaborative, especially around niches and everyone is looking to solve same problems. The speed of change in digital means that no one has all the answers and we need to get comfortable with the not knowing.

As a specialist you will be able to spott opportunities that others miss - see the value you can add and push for it. Write a business case, get a sponsor to help make it happen if you need to, and show what you can do.

"Surround yourself with people that share your values, your vision and ambition and that can do things that you can't. I am regularly in awe of my team and learn from them daily."

Suzi Watford

EVP and CMO

"If you've built a reputation in project management and delivery, resource management and operations positions can be a good sideways move when having a family, rather than a complete career break. Non-client facing delivery roles are easier to handle from home and fit better around the odd hours that mothers with small children can work."

Clare Midgley

Operations Manager

"Master the art of active listening. Be a learn-it-all, not a know-it-all!"

Denise Law

Head of Strategic Product Development

"I used to worry a lot about whether I was creative enough. Then a very successful friend told me that she knew she was never going to be the most creative person in the room, but she could be the most efficient and best prepared, and the easiest to work with. This has really helped me at various points in my career, when I have seriously doubted myself."

Sarah

Editor

How to innovate and think like a disruptor

"People told me 'You won't like it when you go off into the commercial world, it's going to be tough for you'. It was tough. The important thing is to focus on what you bring to the business, the skills, and the fun and the projects that you want to work on."

Kate Bradshaw

10 Digital Ladies Innovator Award winner 2017

Kate Bradshaw is Vice President, Digital Strategy, for the international division of Scripps Networks Interactive. She is responsible for the digital strategy across EMEA, AsiaPac and LatAm. Her role spans content, monetisation, products, processes and a double dose of digital transformation.

SOMETHING IN YOUR BUSINESS NEEDS TO CHANGE BUT YOU'RE AFRAID to speak up? Are you struggling to find new, creative solutions to a problem? Trust your abilities and use these hacks to become a more disruptive thinker and inject fresh ideas into your workplace and career. Remember: you don't have to do it all on your own; start by learning and emulating others whose approach and thinking you admire. If you're trying to innovate or introduce change, think about it from the opposite perspective - how would you want it handled if it affected you but you were not the instigator?

The rewards of taking the risk and being able to push yourself to somewhere where you are quite uncomfortable, is hugely beneficial, even if it doesn't feel like it at the time.

The important thing is to focus on what you bring to the business and the skills and the fun and the projects that YOU want to work on.

Be brave enough to speak up when you know something's not working. The longer you leave it, the more the problem will cost the business and your reputation.

"Trust your gut and trust the process; persevere, even if it's only a step at a time but do not sit still, no matter what doubts or worries you might have."

Katherine Alexander-Dobrovolskaia

Leadership Coach

"Never stop searching for new knowledge and bring everyone on board to share and communicate. Most innovative teams know how to improvise and find new ways of solving problems by playing off each other's contributions. Great outcomes are never solo work. Listen deeply and be a constant and humble learner for more effective and innovative work."

Clara Llamas

Strategist, Researcher and Entrepreneur

"You don't know what you need to know until something doesn't look or feel right. The key is to trust your instinct. Find out what is wrong, fast and put it right."

Suzanne Reece

Education coach, Solicitor (non-practising) and Business Owner

"Don't be afraid to put your ideas forward. If you spot an opportunity to do something differently, speak up and be brave enough to try. Some of my best career moves came from ideas that initially raised eyebrows."

Jessica Hall

User Experience Leader

"Say what you mean - don't compromise what you're trying to say for the sake of diplomacy. Sometimes, ripping off the bandaid or getting straight to the point will save a lot of time and unnecessary conversations."

Keran

Head of Event Content

Working as a consultant

"I make a point of spending three to five hours a week just keeping up-to-date on what's happening in digital innovation. I always need to understand enough of the technology especially to know what's possible and where things are heading."

Tara Hein-Phillips

10 Digital Ladies Consultant Award winner 2017

Tara Hein-Phillips is Managing Director of Vestar Consulting. She has spent the past 13 years running her own consultancy and currently spends 25% of her time as a strategic consultant advising US and UK-based tech start-ups, 50% of her time working with mission-driven organisations to help them to develop sustainable digital growth plans, and 25% of her time working with large global corporations to innovate and change their organisations.

T HE LIFE OF A CONSULTANT CAN OFFER HUGE VARIETY, A CHANCE TO dip in and out of multiple businesses, sectors and workplaces, and the freedom of not being "on staff". But it can present enormous challenges too, whether that's drumming up new clients or handling difficult ones. The good news is there's lots of brilliant digital consultants out there willing to share their hacks on everything from managing client expectations, negotiating rates to pitching and balancing your workload.

Let's start with the advice of our award-winner Tara Hein-Phillips and the brilliant consultancy minds of:

Nici Phoenix Malamoglou *has a passion for disruptive customer engagement and is the Founder of customer engagement consultancy The Tipping Point.*

Sally Foote *is a co-founder of 10 Digital Ladies and previously ran boutique product development consultancy FEB, which worked with some of the UK's biggest media brands*

Ann Longley *is a digital transformation consultant and Founder of Something New Together. She helps brands discover their purpose, tell their stories and transform and future-proof their businesses.*

Be yourself and figure out what you uniquely offer. Get really clear about that offer: who you are, what you do, you have to list it in, say, three bullet points in a way that people will remember. There might not be an opening for you right away, but if prospective clients can remember those three points and understand your methodology, they may call you in future.

Selling isn't a dirty word — every coffee every conversation with a prospective client is time you're not billing for, so you have to get really good at it. Talk about money from the start: ask 'have you got budget?' There's no point you doing three coffees and a pitch deck if there's no budget.

Spend time within a company observing strengths and weaknesses, then pitch how your skill set can make a difference. You'll need to be clear about exactly what your vision is, how it benefits the business and where you fit in but if you get it right they will be excited too.

"My career hack would be trust yourself to try freelancing. You really get to understand your value better. As you have to determine a daily rate for yourself, it's scary but really rewarding too."

Ekua

Founder of DrinksBot

"If it's not your circus, they're not your monkeys."

Angela

Consultant (quoting 10 Digital Ladies Co-Founder Sally Foote)

"Have a list of people you trust who deliver the same service as you. Then, if you can't take a project, you'll still be able to recommend a solution to your client - and if you're lucky your contacts will return the favour."

Babs Guthrie

Digital Consultant

"Presenting and pitching to a client is the same as conducting an orchestra: it's down to you to take them along the right path. Just make sure it's an engaging journey. There's nothing worse than someone speaking in a monotone voice."

Sara Whalen

Head of KAM

Taking a seat on the board

"My advice to people starting out is you should be happy with who you are. Be happy that you are female and you have skills and that you are different sometimes in male-dominated teams. Be confident and try to make the most of the situation."

Christina Scott

10 Digital Ladies Board Member Award winner 2017

Christina Scott is Chief Technology Officer for News UK and Deputy CTO at News Corp. Christina has more than 20 years' experience across the media, IT and engineering industries, and a track record of designing and delivering sophisticated commercial and editorial services and innovations.

I F GETTING TO BOARD LEVEL IS YOUR GOAL, THESE HACKS WILL HELP you get there. Your eyes may be on the prize, but our experts recommend taking a step back and finding the right role and board for you. If that's not your ambition, there's still much to learn from how the best boardroom leaders conduct themselves at work, in meetings and in business.

These hacks include insights from award winner Christina Scott, as well as:

Claire Davenport is CEO at HelloFresh. She started her career as an investment banker for Goldman Sachs and JP Morgan, before taking leadership roles within fast-moving businesses, including Head of Strategy for RTL Group, Chief Commercial Officer at Bigpoint and Chief of Staff at Skype.

Celia Frances is CEO of Rated People, the UK's largest online trade recommendation service, with more than 2 million jobs submitted to-date. Prior to this Celia has held board roles at a number of other organisations, including WeeWorld.

Annabel Shorter has worked as a senior business development executive across a number of large and small organisations and brings more than a decade of negotiating and commercial experience to her clients at Scotwork.

Not all boards are created equal: whether a board position would offer you more influence, recognition or money depends on the organisation. Think about what drives you and the responsibilities you want and find the positions that best suit that. The board is not necessarily the only or best option available to you.

Who you work for and with is critical in developing a strong leadership style. We can often end up emulating those who've managed us in the past. It's important to pay attention to what makes a good manager, director or CEO, and what doesn't.

Doing non-executive roles can help you in an executive role: it gives you breadth. It's stimulating to think about big issues from completely different angles and take lessons from industry to industry.

Consciously go after skills to make you more rounded in order to understand how what you offer fits the organisation's bigger picture. The board is like any team, it works best when there's a variety of different people working together.

"Don't wait for anyone to open a door for you. You don't need permission to knock and that can-do attitude will carry you a very long way."

Kim Guest

In a male-dominated environment, it's easy to feel like you should be spending all your time focusing on goals and achieving results. But time spent building relationships and connecting with others always pays off. The relationships you build will help you through tough times, and will enable you to achieve more in the end.

Jenny Mulholland

Public Sector Account Manager

"Your age and gender do not appear on your CV, neither should they even come to your mind in the meeting room. You are just as good as your ability to combine expertise and soft skills. That is all that matters and that is what makes you a convincing professional with a potential for a great career."

Diane de Fontaine Vive Curtaz

Global Digital Marketing Manager

"Trust your instincts and be bold. You'll be surprised how much jargon is used in the business that just doesn't make sense and is convoluted. Act confident and don't be afraid to ask someone to explain themselves. Other people in the room will secretly thank you for speaking out about what they are thinking."

Marina Cheal

Chief Marketing Officer

Thank you to everyone in the fabulous 10 Digital Ladies community who to took the time to send in advice. We're only sorry we didn't have space to include it all.

Benedicte Autret, Abba Newbery, Alexandra Wyatt, Alison Rood, Amy Wilson, Andrew Moughtin-Mumby, Angela, Anja Maerz, Ann Holman, Anna Carus-Wilson, Ariane Bernard, Babita Earle, Babs Guthrie, Camille Peetroons, Carrie Birmingham, Catriona Bolger, Chandreyi Saha, Charlotte Peters, Cheryl Clements, Chrissy Silva, Clara Llamas, Clare Midgley, Denise Law, Diane de Fontaine Vive Curtaz, Ekua Cant, Emma Farrow, Emma Sinden, Farida Lodhi, Fiona, Flora Graham, Flora Okumagba, Francine, Gabriella Lee, Gaby Jesson, Ghilaine Chan, Hannah Bowden, Heather Carr, Helen Unwjn, Imola Unger,

Inga Thordar, Jane, Jenni, Jenny Mulholland, Jessica Hall, Juliet Eccleston,

Karen Ortiz-McAvoy, Kate Thompson , Katherine Alexander-Dobrovolskaia

Keran, Kim Guest, Kim Rowell, Laura Robinson, Lauren Howells, Lauren Maffeo,

Lauren Murray, Lexie Papaspyrou, Marika Clemow, Marina Cheal, Matilde Giglio,

Melissa McVeigh, Neelam Parmar, Nina Lovelace, Penelope Jones, Qing Mak,

Rebecca McIntosh, Reshma Shaikh, Sara Whalen, Sarah, Sarah Arnold, Sarah

Marshall, Sarah Stokes, Sass Allard, Shoshana Bloom, Stephanie Fletcher, Suzanne

Reece, Suzi Watford, Tanya Alden, Tessa Cooper, Tiffany Charters, Zoe Whitman.